SCARY ORIGAMI

Written by
Jill Smolinski

Illustrated by Anita McLaughlin

Lowell House
Juvenile
Los Angeles

CONTEMPORARY BOOKS
Chicago

Publisher: Jack Artenstein
Vice President/General Manager, Juvenile Division: Elizabeth Amos
Director of Publishing Services: Rena Copperman
Editorial Director: Brenda Pope-Ostrow
Senior Editor: Amy Downing
Art Director: Lisa-Theresa Lenthall
Crafts Artist: Charlene Olexiewicz
Cover Photo: Ann Bogart

Lowell House books can be purchased at special discounts when ordered in bulk for premiums and special sales.
Contact Department JH at the following address:

Lowell House Juvenile
2029 Century Park East, Suite 3290
Los Angeles, CA 90067

Library of Congress Catalogue Card Number: 95-21112

ISBN: 1-56565-353-X

10 9 8 7 6 5 4 3 2

CONTENTS

BEFORE you start

Who's afraid of a stack of paper?
You might be surprised! Just as the dark shadows of the night
can seem to hide a hideous monster in your room, somewhere
within a simple square of paper there may be a ghoul just waiting
to be set free. How would you like to fold up a bloodthirsty bat?
Or a headless corpse? Or a haunted ship setting sail?
No matter what you choose, you can create a collection of
creatures so creepy, they'll send you screaming for your mummy!

WHAT YOU'LL NEED

Any thin, square paper can be used to fold your forms. You can buy special origami paper at art supply and specialty stores that is colored on one side, white on the other, and precut into squares. Paper sizes will vary depending on the craft. Most of the designs in this book can be made with materials you can find around the house.

BASIC FOLDS

There are three basic folds you will need to know.

Valley Fold

Fold the paper toward you.

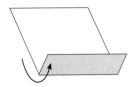

Mountain Fold

Fold the paper away from you.

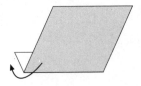

Squash Fold

This fold is usually called for when two sides of a flap need to be squashed flat. To do it, poke your finger inside the flap and—you guessed it—squash it.

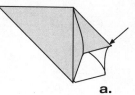 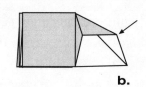

a.   b.

BASIC FORMS

The jack-o'-lantern on page 24 and the vampire on page 26 may look very different, but both start with the same basic form. Here you'll learn the forms that are the foundations for many of the projects you'll make.

Basic Form 1

1 Begin with a piece of origami paper in a flat diamond shape, color side face down. Fold your paper in half, bringing the left point to meet the right point, then unfold to make a crease.

2 Now fold the left and right sides to the center line so your paper looks like a kite.

Basic Form 2

1 Begin with a piece of origami paper in a flat diamond shape, color side face down. Fold your paper in half, bringing the bottom point to meet the top.

2 Now fold the far left and right points up to the center so the points meet at the top of your form.

Basic Form 3

1 Begin with a square piece of paper, color side face down (unless otherwise specified). Fold the paper in half by bringing the top edge to meet the bottom edge, then fold it in half again by folding the left side to meet the right side. Reopen it into a square.

2 Next, fold each of the four corners to the center point, where the two creases made in Step 1 cross.

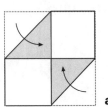 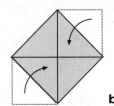
a. b.

Basic Form 4

1 To make this form, you need to follow the first step in Basic Form 3, then unfold. Fold it diagonally both ways. Reopen it.

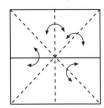

2 Fold the top half of the paper to meet the bottom half to make a rectangle. Then fold the left side to meet the right side so you have a square. The square should have the open ends facing down and to the right.

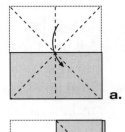
a.

b.

3 Hold the top flap up straight and poke your finger inside until it reaches the very tip. Carefully squash the flap down to form a triangle. Be sure all your corners line up and look pointed.

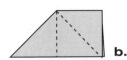
a. b.

4 Turn the form over and repeat this step on the other side.

Basic Form 5

1 To make this form, follow the first step 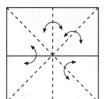 in Basic Form 3, then unfold. Fold it diagonally both ways. Reopen it.

2 Lay it in a diamond shape in front of you, and fold the paper in half, bringing the top point down to meet the bottom point.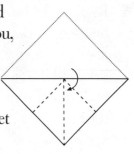

3 Carefully hold the right side of the form open at point A, then squash-fold it by pushing down on it to meet point B.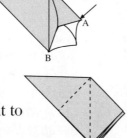

4 Repeat Step 3 with the left side of the form.

Basic Form 6

1 Begin with your paper in a square, 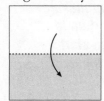 then fold it in half, bringing the top edge to meet the bottom edge.

2 Fold the rectangle-shaped form in half again by bringing the left side to meet the right, make a crease, then unfold. 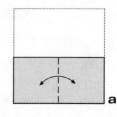 Now fold the right side to meet the center crease. Do the same with the left side.

3 Lift the left side up at a 90-degree angle, then squash-fold it so it forms the shape of a house. Repeat this step on the right side.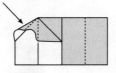

Basic Form 7

1 Begin with your paper folded with the first step in Basic Form 3, then unfold it so it is lying flat. Fold the right and left sides so they meet the center line.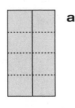

2 Now fold the bottom and top edges so they meet the center line. Make a nice sharp crease, then unfold it.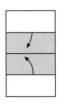

3 Your form should now look like this. Make two diagonal creases across the center four squares

a.

only. Do this first by folding point A to meet point B. Crease the paper sharply, then unfold it. Now

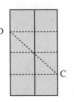
b.

repeat this step on the opposite side, bringing point C to meet point D.

c.

4 This next step is tricky, so look closely at the illustration for help. First, grasp the bottom two corners. Then lift them up and gently tug them apart so they flatten and the bottom edge meets the center. Repeat this step with the top two corners, only this time pull them down to meet the center.

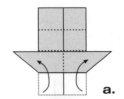
a.

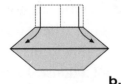
b.

TIPS FOR THE FAINTHEARTED

Origami is supposed to be fun—so don't feel bad if the projects you make from this book only look frightening at first because they're so lumpy or crooked. The more you practice, the easier it gets. Always work on a smooth, hard surface and make each crease as straight as possible. If you make a mistake, chalk it up to experience and start over with a new piece of paper.

A VERY HAUNTED house

Be it ever so creepy, there's no place like home.

WHAT YOU'LL NEED

**light-colored origami paper • markers • scissors
cotton swabs • black marker**

DIRECTIONS

1 Begin with Basic Form 4. Fold the lower left and right corners (front flaps only) up to the center point. Turn the form over and repeat this step on the other side.

2 Take the front flap and its leftmost point and squash-fold it by inserting your finger until it touches the corner, then pressing it flat so it forms a square. Repeat this step with the right point. Your form should be in the shape of a simple house. Turn it over and repeat this step on the other side.

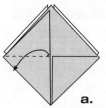 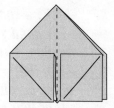

a.   b.

3 Fold the left and right sides in to touch the middle, forming two creases. Then unfold.

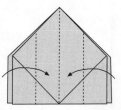

4 Using a mountain fold, fold back the front flap of the right and left sides. Then flip the form over and repeat this step on the other side.

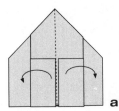

a.

b.

5 Fold points C and D down to make a crease, then unfold.

6 Poke your finger into the tip of point C and squash-fold it. It should look like a tiny house. Repeat this step with point D. Turn the form over and repeat this step.

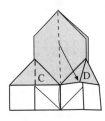

7 Lift up the center bottom point (pointing toward you) until it's even with the other two roofs and pointing away from you. Secure this short roof by gluing it to the rest of the structure. Your house is almost ready for its unearthly inhabitants.

TERRIFYING TIP

Make a spooky scene to surround your haunted mansion. First, glue your form flat to a piece of black cardboard. Then cut or tear construction paper in eerie shapes, like tombstones, ghosts, a full moon, and bats, and glue them around your house.

8 Use scissors to cut four lines (front flaps only) as shown in the illustration. Fold the two new flaps to the center to form a pair of shutters.

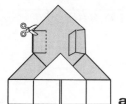 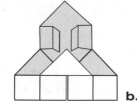

a.   b.

9 Draw doors and windows on your house. Cut cotton swabs in half, then use a fine-tip marker to draw ghostly faces on the cotton tips. Poke holes with a pen point in the windows of your house, and insert the stick portion of the ghosts so that they sit inside.

BEASTLY
wolf

A dark night. A full moon. Thick, black clouds. It's the perfect setting for bringing to life a very hairy—and scary—werewolf.

WHAT YOU'LL NEED

brown origami paper • pink construction paper • brown and black yarn glue • scissors • rice • markers

DIRECTIONS

1 Lay the piece of origami in a diamond shape, color side face down. Form a triangle with the fold at the top by bringing the top point down to meet the bottom point.

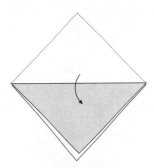

2 To form the werewolf's ears, fold the left and right points down, about ½ inch higher than the bottommost point. Take the top ½ inch of the paper and fold it behind, then fold the bottommost point back about ½ inch. The werewolf's head should be taking shape.

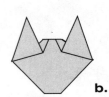

3 Continue your werewolf by folding part of the ear up so that it stands up above his head in a sharp point. Repeat this step on the opposite ear.

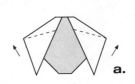

4 Draw in yellow eyes, a nose, and a mouth. Glue white rice in a triangular pattern near the mouth to form fearsome fangs. Cut the pink construction paper in the shape of large almonds to decorate the ears. Glue brown and black yarn spread out all over his face to make the creature really hairy.

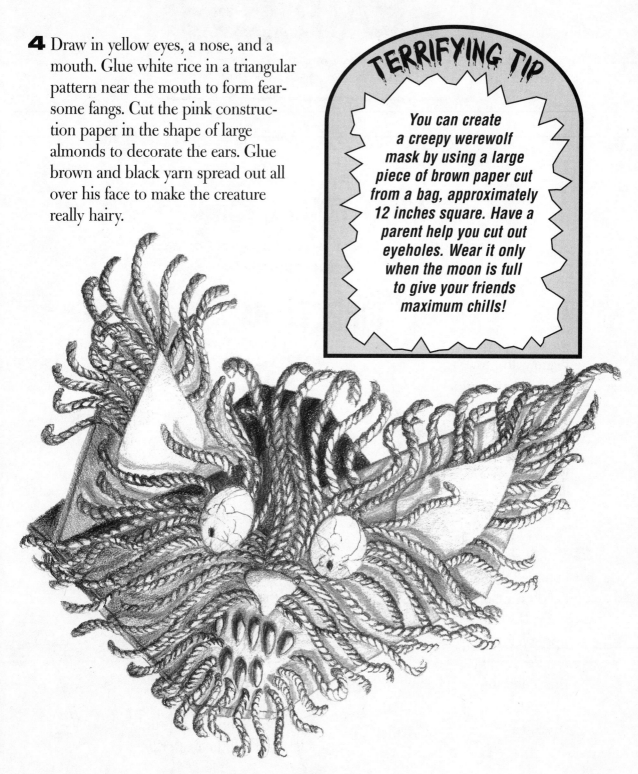

HEADLESS corpse

Watch this body fold its way into existence—but wait!
Where is its head?

WHAT YOU'LL NEED

light-colored origami paper • markers or paints
Ping-Pong ball • glue • tiny buttons • yarn

DIRECTIONS

1 Begin with Basic Form 1 (open side face down), then use a mountain fold to bring the top point back and down to meet the bottom point.

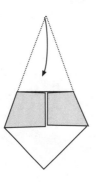

2 Next, lift point A straight up and flatten the right side of the form, then repeat this step with the left side of the form.

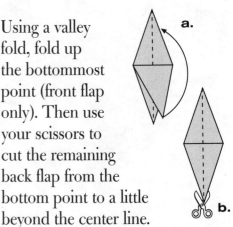

3 You've almost completed the headless man's body. Fold the upper left and right edges in to the center line.

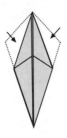

4 Using a valley fold, fold up the bottommost point (front flap only). Then use your scissors to cut the remaining back flap from the bottom point to a little beyond the center line.

14

5 Turn your form over and carefully fold the left and right points to the center line.

6 Are you ready to make the headless man's arms? Simply fold out each point as shown in the illustration. Tuck the center point between the main body folds. It's headless!

7 Turn your form over and fold the arms out in front of the body. Fold the feet up.

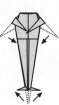

8 Color a pair of pants on the lower portion of the body. Glue on tiny buttons, and with a red marker, color a bloodstain down the front of its shirt. To make the head, take the Ping-Pong ball and paint a face on it, either tortured or silly. Glue some yarn on it for hair, then glue the ball in between the corpse's hands.

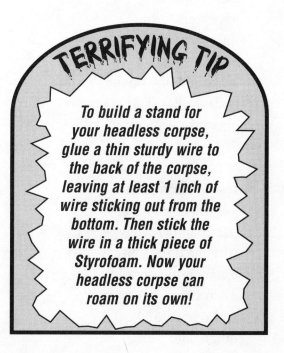

TERRIFYING TIP

To build a stand for your headless corpse, glue a thin sturdy wire to the back of the corpse, leaving at least 1 inch of wire sticking out from the bottom. Then stick the wire in a thick piece of Styrofoam. Now your headless corpse can roam on its own!

Pretty to look at, but don't get too close. This plant has nasty fangs and a never-ending thirst for blood.

WHAT YOU'LL NEED

two sheets of red origami paper • red ribbon • bendable straw
markers • scissors • tape • glue

DIRECTIONS

1 Start with Basic Form 5 (with the colored side face up). When you have your form, the color should be on the *inside*. Make sure the open ends (or flaps) are pointed upward, away from you.

2 Find the points on the right and left sides (front flap only), and fold them to the center line. Turn over and repeat on the other side.

3 Use a valley fold to fold each lower corner as shown, making sure the points just touch in the middle. Turn your form over and repeat on the other side.

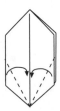

4 Fold the entire form in half to make a crease, then open. Use your scissors to cut straight across the bottom to make a tiny hole.

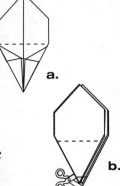

a.

b.

5 Now you're ready to let your flower bloom! Using the illustration as a guide, gently tug the petals open. Bend each one back at the crease. Poke your finger inside the middle of the flower so the petals no longer meet in the center.

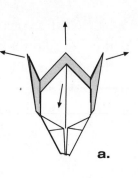

a.

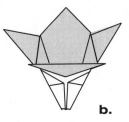

b.

6 It doesn't look very scary yet, does it? To make a fiend out of your flower, you must first make a second flower by repeating Steps 1–5 with another piece of paper. When it's finished, tuck it inside the first one, with the petals *not* aligning with the first flower's petals. Secure it in place with some dots of glue.

7 To give your flower razor-sharp teeth (the better to eat you with, my dear!), fold the top and bottom points inward. When you do this, it will expose the white side. Using your scissors, make jagged cuts as shown— and your pretty petals suddenly turn into terrible teeth.

TERRIFYING TIP

Display your biting beauty in a clear glass on which you've taped a note that warns, "Beware . . . Don't Feed Me!"

8 Cut a 3-inch piece of red ribbon. Tuck it in your flower's mouth and down through the hole at the bottom so it looks like a tongue. Use markers to draw eyes on the petals just above your flower's fangs. Finally, make a stem by taping your flower to a straw. (It will be easier to do this if you insert the straw slightly into the hole at the bottom of the flower.)

Beware! Don't Feed Me

BLOODSUCKING
black widow

She perches on a ghostly web, waiting for her next victim.

WHAT YOU'LL NEED

three sheets of black origami paper • pencil • puff paint
popcorn kernels • glue • scissors

DIRECTIONS

1 Begin by folding the paper diagonally into a triangle. Open it. Placing the paper in front of you, fold the top point and its left edge to the center line. Take the bottom point and its right edge and fold it to the center line.

2 Take the new bottom point and its left edge and fold it to the center, and take the top point and right edge and fold it to the center.

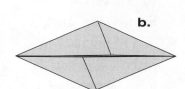

3 You now have a diamond shape. Fold this in half by bringing the top point over to meet the bottom.

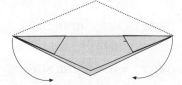

4 Use a pencil to make tiny dots about a third of the way in from each end. Then use a valley fold to bring points on the right and left sides forward, bending them at the spot you just marked. Crease them well, then use a mountain fold and re-fold them down the back side.

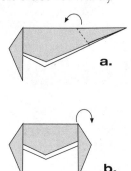

a.

b.

5 The body and legs are starting to take shape! Make your spider sturdier by using an inside-reverse fold to tuck her legs into her body. To do this, lift the point on the right side out as shown, and poke it inside the body. Do the same with the left side.

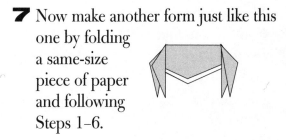

a.

b.

6 Pull the point on the right side back out so it forms a kite shape. Using scissors, cut up the middle to the top of the leg—and now you have two! Repeat this step on the left side. Tuck everything back in place and flatten the form by pressing gently on it.

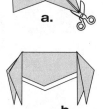

a.

b.

7 Now make another form just like this one by folding a same-size piece of paper and following Steps 1–6.

8 Take a third piece of origami paper that's approximately half the size you used for the other pieces of the spider's body. Fold it in half by folding the top point to meet the bottom.

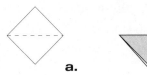

a.

b.

9 Assemble your black widow by gluing the two body pieces together so that the "back" of one body is glued to the "front" of the other. Then take the triangle-shaped flap you made in Step 8 and lay it over the top of the body so it covers it like a shawl. Glue it in place.

a.

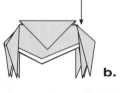

b.

10 Glue on popcorn kernels for eyes, and use puff paint to draw a mouth and fangs. Paint a red hourglass shape at the top of your spider's back—the telltale mark of the deadly black widow.

TERRIFYING TIP

To make a web, start with a square of white paper. Fold it in half, then in half again. Use scissors to cut shapes along the folded edges, being careful not to cut away any edge entirely. When you unfold the paper, you'll have a willowy web. Hang your spider from the web with white string.

FLYING witch

When the midnight bell tolls, it's the witching hour—time for witches everywhere to hop on their broomsticks and soar into the night sky.

WHAT YOU'LL NEED

origami paper (black on both sides) • green construction paper
scissors • glue • markers

DIRECTIONS

1 Start with your paper in a square. Fold it in half to make a crease by bringing the top edge to the bottom, then unfold. Now fold the top side to the center line to make a crease, and unfold.

2 Fold the lower left corner so it touches the top crease. Now fold the upper left corner so it over- laps the previous fold and forms a point.

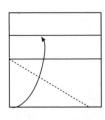

a.

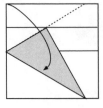

b.

3 Turn your form over, with the point on the right side and the flat edge on the left side. Fold the right point back to the left edge.

a.

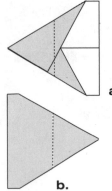

b.

4 Now fold the point part of the way back, overlapping the right edge about 2 inches.

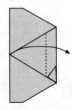

5 To make your witch's hat, start with point A, squash-folding the flap to the center crease. When you do this, the little valley fold at the side will form itself. Repeat this step on point B.

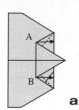

a.

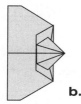

b.

6 Fold the left and right sides of the witch's hat into the center. Fold it in half with a mountain fold along the center crease. Then fold each side of the cape down to meet the middle. Finally, fold up about ½ inch on each side of the cape to help your witch soar.

a.

b.

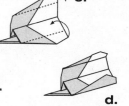

c.

d.

7 Complete your witch by cutting out a small circle of green construction paper and drawing a horrid witch's face on it. Glue the face in the area under the hat. Be sure to glue it on securely so it doesn't come undone when you send your witch flying. Now you're ready to launch your witch into the dark night!

Face your jack-o'-lantern one way to give anyone a bad dream.
Turn it around, and it's enough to cause a nightmare!

WHAT YOU'LL NEED

orange origami paper • markers • green pipe cleaner

DIRECTIONS

1 Begin with Basic Form 4 and fold the lower left and right corners (front flaps only) to the center, then turn the form over and repeat this step.

2 Now fold the front flaps of the right and left points to the center line. Turn the form over again and repeat this step on the other side.

3 Fold and unfold points A and B (front flaps only) to make a sharp crease.

4 Next, tuck points A and B into the center triangles as shown. To do this, open the triangle pockets with your fingers and slip the edge in.

5 Turn your form over and repeat Steps 3 and 4 on the other side.

6 Pick up the right flap and close it as though you were turning the page of a book. The plain side of the form should now be showing. Turn the form over and repeat.

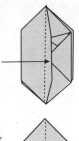
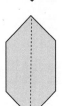

7 Use markers to draw a scary face on your jack-o'-lantern. Then, on the other side, draw an even *more* frightening face. Find the tiny hole at the bottom of your form. When you blow into it, your pumpkin will puff up right before your eyes.

8 Stick an inch-long piece of green pipe cleaner in its top for a stem.

TERRIFYING TIP

Cut a hole in the top of your jack-o'-lantern to hold candy corn, gummy worms, or even cooked pumpkin seeds!

MIDNIGHT stalker

Is someone you know actually a bloodsucking vampire?

WHAT YOU'LL NEED

black origami paper • scissors • glue • photograph • red puff paint • white-out

DIRECTIONS

1 Start with Basic Form 4. Using the illustration as a guide, fold the front right side flap to cover the left side. Then fold the right flap in half to meet the center of your form.

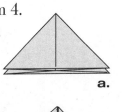

a.

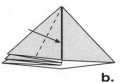

b.

2 Bring the folded flap back to the right side where you started. That's half the vampire's body.

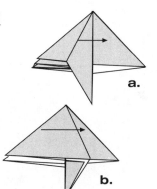

a.

b.

3 Now, take the front left flap and fold it over to the right side. Then fold the left flap in half to meet the center of the form. Bring the folded flap back to the left side.

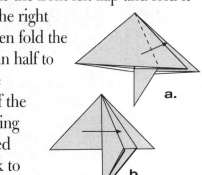

a.

b.

4 Use a mountain fold to fold back the corners of sides A and B approximately ½ inch.

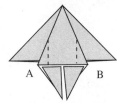

A   B

5 Use scissors to make tiny cuts as you see here. Then fold the top point down to form a hairline. Your vampire's collar and ears will stick up on either side. To make feet, fold the very tips of the bottom points up ½ inch.

a.

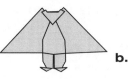

b.

6 Now it's time to reveal the secret identity of your vampire. Find a spare photograph of someone you know where his or her head is about the size of a nickel. You'll have to cut the photo, so be sure to ask your parents if it's okay to use it. (If you don't have a photograph, you can use a picture from a magazine.) Cut out the face, then use white-out to paint fangs on the person's mouth. Glue the face on the front of your vampire, just underneath the hairline. Or, use the origami head part as a hood and glue on the picture so it's peeking out from under the hood.

7 Drizzle a thin line of red puff paint down from one of the fangs onto the body of your vampire to look like dripping blood.

8 Hide the secret identity of your vampire by folding the wings across its body.

TERRIFYING TIP

If you like to read scary books, why not let this toothy terror hold your place? Just slide a Popsicle stick up the opening in the back of your vampire's cape and tape it in place.

ANCIENT tombstones

These terrifying headstones mark the spot where the living dead make their home.

WHAT YOU'LL NEED

gray origami paper • black pen

DIRECTIONS

1 Begin with your paper in a square. Fold the left and right sides about an inch in from the edges. Then use a valley fold to fold the form in half, bringing the top to the bottom.

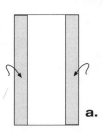

a.

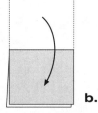

b.

2 Fold the form in half once more, this time bringing the left side to meet the right. Then unfold your form to make the crease as shown. Use a valley fold to bring each side to the middle crease, then unfold.

a.

b.

3 Make two more creases by folding and unfolding the top left and right points.

4 Now open the left side slightly. Push down on the left corner and tuck the fold inside. Repeat this step with the right corner.

a.

b.

5 A black pen is all you need to mark this grave. With big block letters, write R.I.P., which stands for Rest In Peace. Then make up ghastly names like Frank N. Stein or Vanna Pire. Be sure to include the date of death and maybe a mysterious message, such as See You Soon!

TERRIFYING TIP

Planning a party so fun it could raise the dead? Let guests know about it with tombstone invitations. Include all the details, like the date, time, and location, and instead of R.I.P., write R.T.P., which means Ready To Party!

PSYCHO cyclops

This folded fiend has just one eyeball, but mortals beware . . .
he may have his eye on you!

WHAT YOU'LL NEED

origami paper • marble • scissors • glue • white-out • red marker

DIRECTIONS

1 Begin with Basic Form 2, and lay the form in front of you so the two loose flaps are pointed toward you, face up. Fold the two bottom front flaps up to the tip of the form.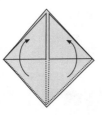

2 Now fold the left tip of the front flap out as shown. Repeat this step on the right tip.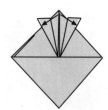

3 Use a mountain fold to fold back the points on the right and left sides, as well as the top point.

4 To make your cyclops's nose, fold the bottom point (front flap only) up to the widest part, then back down about ½ inch.

5 Use your scissors to carefully make tiny cuts as shown. This will give your cyclops saw-edged teeth.

6 Tuck the back flap of the bottom point inside the form to make a chin.

7 Are you ready to give your ghoul the eye? First, carefully paint the top two triangular shapes using white-out. Once it dries, draw thin squiggly red lines to look like veins.

8 Gently push down on the top of the form's head—this will make a round hole between the pieces you just painted. Dab some glue inside and insert a marble. The bloodshot white of the eye should fold around it, holding it in place just like an eye socket. Be sure to let your monster dry completely before letting it roam free.

TERRIFYING TIP

Keep an eye on your papers by making your cyclops into a paperweight. Don't set a marble in the eye socket. Instead, in the hole put the largest rock that you can find that will fit. Your papers will be virtually paralyzed by its one-eyed, stony *stare*.

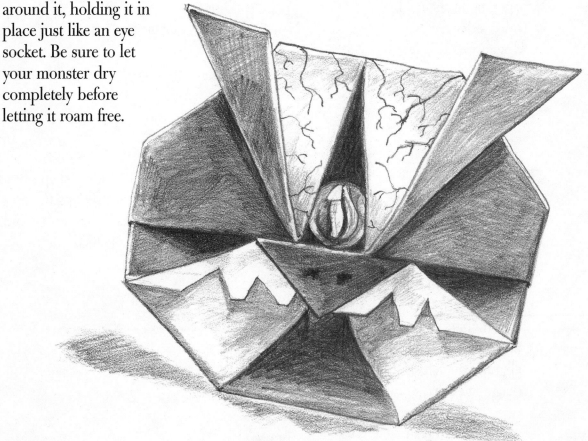

GRUESOME ghost

Ooooooo-ooohh! Don't let this frightening spook catch you unawares!

WHAT YOU'LL NEED

white origami paper • black marker • scissors

DIRECTIONS

1 Begin with Basic Form 2, with the opening in the back, open sides facing downward. Then fold the upper right and left edges in to meet at the center line.

2 Unfold the back flaps. These will soon be the ghost's arms.

3 Fold the left point over to the right so the edge facing up is a straight horizontal line. The left point should extend beyond the form slightly. Crease it well, then fold it back to the left, aligning the left diagonal edges.

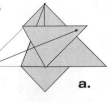

a.

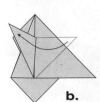

b.

4 There should be a small strip of paper from this fold that overlaps the crease into the right area. Use a valley fold to fold it over to the left side of the crease.

5 Repeat Steps 3 and 4 for the right side.

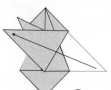

a.   **b.**   **c.**

6 Using scissors, cut a wavy line as shown along each of the arms. Turn the form over.

7 Your form should have three layers: the front layer that is the head and body, a small second layer, and a third layer, which makes the arms. Take the left side of the second layer, and using a valley fold, tuck it behind the first layer. Do the same thing with the right side.

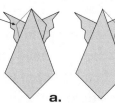

a.   **b.**

TERRIFYING TIP

The loud clanging of chains is a sign that an evil spirit is near. To make a chain for your ghost, string together paper clips (the smaller the better), then lay them around the creature's arms and body.

8 Draw eerie eyes and a mouth on your spirit's face. Give the tip of the head a slight twist. Use a mountain fold to turn back the bottom point. This will form a stand that allows your ghost to float on its own. Gently spread out the arms to give the effect that the ghost is attacking!

CURSED
evil mummy

When it comes to scaring the life out of someone, this mummy has it wrapped up.

WHAT YOU'LL NEED

white origami paper • scissors • white ribbon • black marker • tape

DIRECTIONS

1 Start with Basic Form 1, then use your scissors to make two cuts as shown, about 2 inches below the top (or more if you're using very large paper). Make sure to leave at least an inch between the two slits.

2 Find the points that were formed when you made the cuts, then fold each to the middle so the points overlap each other in a straight horizontal line. This will be the mummy's diamond-shaped head.

3 Look closely at the illustration for this step. Cut a line about ½ inch below the horizontal line where the two sides meet. You'll have to go through all the layers of paper, so snip carefully to make sure your form doesn't tear.

4 Using a valley fold, bring the mummy's head (the top of the form) forward and tuck it all the way into the pocket you just cut. You may have to fold in the sides of the head a bit to get it all the way through. If you do need to fold it, unfold it after you get the head tucked in.

34

5 Now fold the right and left diagonal edges to meet at the center line.

6 Do you see the dotted line on the illustration? Use a valley fold to fold your form at this line. The mummy's head will pop up by itself.

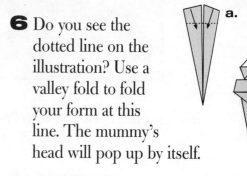

7 Turn your form over and give your mummy a rounded head by using a mountain fold to fold the tip back.

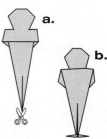

8 Cut a line up the middle from the bottom point to make legs, then fold up the ends an inch or so to create feet.

9 Draw the face. Wind ribbon loosely around the mummy's head and body, taping it in back so it stays in place.

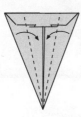

TERRIFYING TIP

Make a Creepo Casket for your mummy (instructions on page 52) using a piece of paper at least twice the size you used to make your mummy—that will give it plenty of room to sleep peacefully.

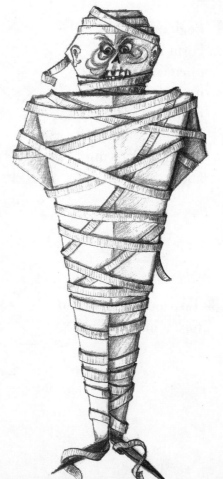

FANGS a lot!

You'll get lots of compliments when you wear this hideous hat.
It looks just like a monster's head!

WHAT YOU'LL NEED

paper about 20 inches square (one side white, if possible) • scissors
poster or puff paint • glue • tape • yarn

DIRECTIONS

1 Begin with Basic Form 2, with the open crease facing up and the open sides facing toward you. Fold the bottom left and right flaps up about two-thirds.

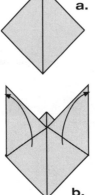

2 Bring the bottom point of the front flap up until it almost reaches the tip of what will be the ghoul's head. Then fold the top third of it back down to make a nose, gluing the flap down.

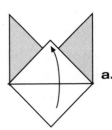

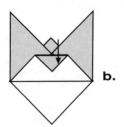

3 Take the back flap and tuck it into the hat.

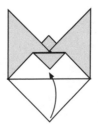

4 Ready to make your monster look more monstrous? First, use scissors to snip out triangles along the bottom front (where the white side shows) to make jagged teeth. If your origami paper is not white on one side, you'll need to paint the teeth white or crusty yellow.

5 Cut strands of yarn about a foot long and gather them in a bunch, tying them in the middle with a shorter piece of yarn, and tape it to the top point of your monster's head like a mop of ratty hair. Paint on two eyes—or more, if you want. Your hat is now ready to wear . . . and scare!

TERRIFYING TIP

Make a mini-version of this hat using ordinary-size origami paper. You can use the hat to disguise dolls, small stuffed animals, or ceramic figurines.

We'll help you make the claws, but you supply the zombie!

WHAT YOU'LL NEED

ten sheets of 2-inch-square green origami paper • black marker
tape • green clay

DIRECTIONS

1 Start with Basic Form 1, then unfold the top flap.

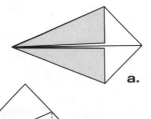

a.

2 Fold the top point down, bending it at the crease line.

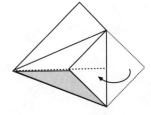

b.

3 Now fold the form in half. As you do this, tuck point B into the pocket at point A. One claw is done! Tape the two sides closed to secure it.

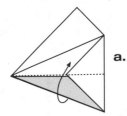

a.

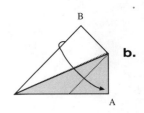

b.

4 Stick it on a finger of the hand you don't write 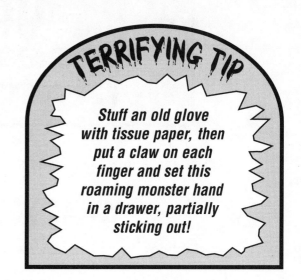 with, putting the paper crease down the middle of your finger. Slightly flatten the area of the claw that extends beyond your finger, then use a black marker to color on a fingernail. Add bumps and warts by pressing on small balls of green clay.

TERRIFYING TIP

Stuff an old glove with tissue paper, then put a claw on each finger and set this roaming monster hand in a drawer, partially sticking out!

5 Make a whole set of ten claws, and stick them on your fingers for a real fright!

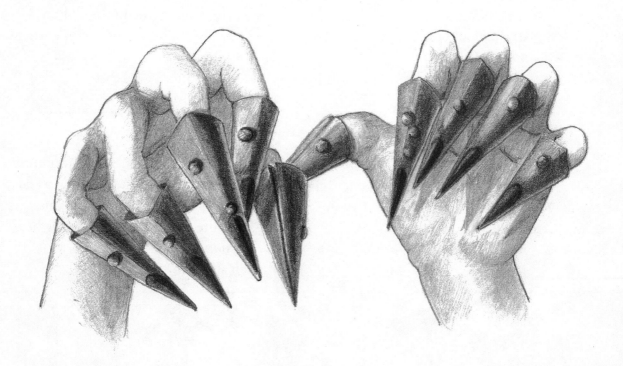

UFO
unidentified flying origami

Just a flick of the wrist sends this UFO into deep space.

WHAT YOU'LL NEED

eight sheets of origami paper • glue • stickers • markers

DIRECTIONS

1 Start with your paper in a square, then fold the bottom half up to meet the top half.

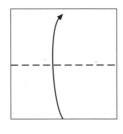

2 Fold the upper left corner so the left side aligns along the bottom of the form. Now fold the lower right corner up so the right side meets the top of the form.

3 You've just made one unit of your UFO. You'll need to make seven more to have enough to build your flying saucer.

4 Tuck the pointed end of one unit into the pocket of another. Push it in as far as it will go and secure it with glue. Make sure you put them in the right direction so they form a circle.

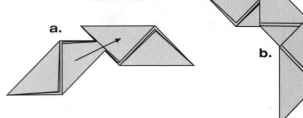

a.

b.

40

5 Use stickers and markers to identify the home base of your alien ship. For example, if it comes from the Long Lost Planet, put on a sticker of a dinosaur, then write the name of the planet on one of the units. Draw a door and windows on other units.

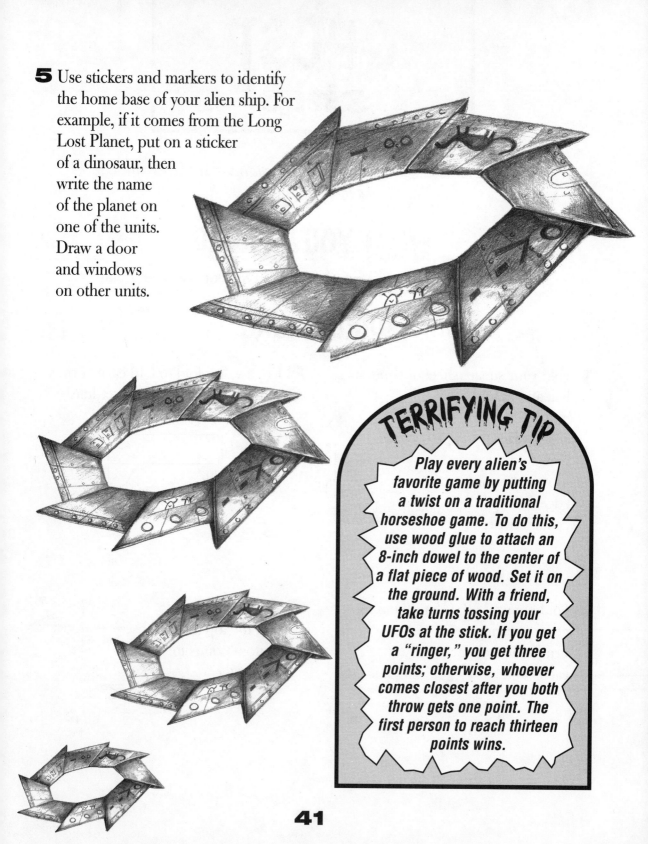

GHOST ship

Out on the night seas, the ghostly remains of sunken ships make their final voyage.

WHAT YOU'LL NEED

brown origami paper • white paper • wooden skewer • clay

DIRECTIONS

1 Fold your square sheet of paper in half and unfold, making sure the color is face up. Now fold the top and bottom edges to the center crease.

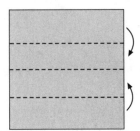

2 Use a valley fold to fold each corner in so the edges meet the center line.

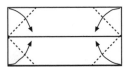

3 Fold points A, B, C, and D to the center, making firm creases on each edge.

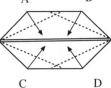

4 Use a valley fold to fold the top and bottom points to the center.

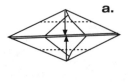

a.

b.

5 To see your ship take shape, you have to flip the form inside out. To do this, pull apart the top and bottom edges at the center line, then push the inner layers up and out, turning the ship inside out. Use your fingers to round out the bottom of your ship and to pinch points on the bow and stern (that's the front and back). You've got it!

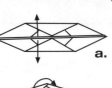
a.

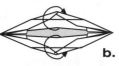
b.

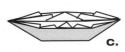
c.

6 Your boat will float better if it has extra weight and some sails. Place a small, flat circle of clay in the bottom of your boat. Tear tissue or parchment paper into three small squares so the edges are ragged. Decorate one of your sails with a skull and crossbones. Poke the paper through the skewer like paper shish kabobs, then set the skewer in the clay.

TERRIFYING TIP

What's a ghost ship without ghosts? Make your own skeletons by gluing white cotton swabs in the shape of a body, arms, and legs (you'll probably have to snap or cut the swabs). Use one of the cotton swab ends for its head. Now carefully set your skeleton in the ship to set sail!

PSYCHOTIC eyeballs

When you keep your eye on the spinning eyeball,
you'll find yourself getting sleepy . . . very, very sleepy . . .

WHAT YOU'LL NEED

two sheets of red origami paper • black paper
glasses • tape or glue • scissors

DIRECTIONS

1 Begin with Basic Form 7, folded so the white part of the paper is on the outside. Do you see the points on the left and right sides of your form? Take the top half of the left point and lift it so it points straight up. Then take the bottom half of the right point and pull it so it points straight down.

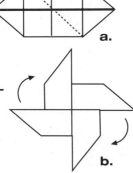

2 Your form should look like a windmill. Now squash-fold one of the points by lifting and opening it out, then squashing it flat so it forms a square. Repeat this step on the other three points.

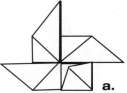

3 Use a valley fold to fold the inner two edges in each square to the center as shown. It should form a tiny triangle with its point to the center of your square. Repeat this step on each of the squares.

4 Now get ready for some serious squashing. Start by lifting one of the small triangular folds up, then opening it slightly and pressing it flat so it looks like a tiny kite, as you see in the illustration. Repeat this step on each of the eight points on your form.

a.

b.

5 You're almost done! Just use a mountain fold to fold back the four corners and you'll have an eyeball staring you in the face.

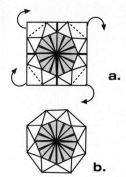

a.

b.

6 Repeat Steps 1–5 to make a second eye. Cut a small circle out of the center of each eyeball. Tape or glue them to a pair of glasses. Put them on—you're sure to freak out friends and family! *(Warning: Don't try skateboarding, in-line skating, bicycling, or any other activity that could cause you to crash while wearing these psycho glasses.)*

TERRIFYING TIP

Add glow-in-the-dark paint to your set of eyes and tape or tack them to your wall. Then, as the sun goes down, you'll get that eerie feeling that someone is watching you!

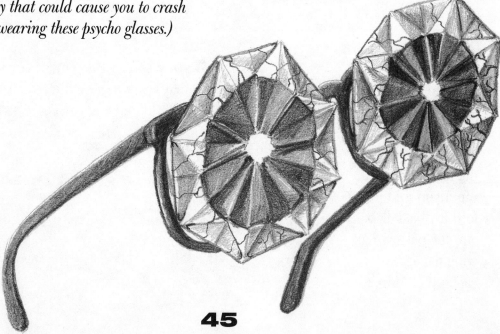

*It's a dark, chilly night. What's that rustling in the trees?
Is it just the wind, or could it be the flapping of a vampire bat's wings
as it swoops down and claims its next unsuspecting victim?*

WHAT YOU'LL NEED

black origami paper • puff paint • scissors • glue • black felt-tip marker

DIRECTIONS

1 Begin with a sheet of paper in a diamond shape, then fold it in half. Now fold the bottom edge halfway up.

2 Turn the form over, and fold down point A (just the front flap) partway. Fold the tip of A back up again. You've just made the body and wings of your bat.

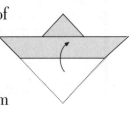

A

3 Fold the form in half. Use a valley fold to fold the front flap on the right to the left, then use a mountain fold to fold the back flap. Are the bat's wings lying flat against each other? Great!

a.

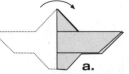
b.

c.

4 Now spread the wings back apart. You may want to glue the area at the back where the wings meet.

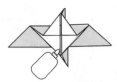

5 To make the bat's head, squash-fold point D by holding the tip and pushing it down flat until it forms a square. Dab some glue inside the head so it lies closer to the body.

6 Using scissors, cut away areas shown by the dotted lines in the illustration. This will form your bat's ears and give a wavy edge to its wings.

7 Secure the head with a dab of glue in the opening, right below the ears. Color any exposed white areas with a black felt-tip marker. Use dots of puff paint to create yellow eyes and a red mouth.

TERRIFYING TIP

Make a creepy version of a Christmas tree for a Halloween decoration. Find a big dead branch with lots of little twigs attached, and set it upright in a pot filled with rocks or sand. Hang a flock of tiny bats from the tree by gluing loops of string to the back of each bat.

FEROCIOUS feline fiend

If you let this black cat slink across your path, be ready for lots of bad luck.

WHAT YOU'LL NEED

black origami paper • white paper • puff paint • pencil • glue

DIRECTIONS

1 Start with Basic Form 1, turning it so the wider half is on the right. Then fold the top and bottom edges on the right to the center line.

2 Fold the form in half top to bottom, and make a crease from point A to the middle of the top edge, point B, as shown. Make sure the crease is sharp and the next step will be easy.

a.

b.

3 Tightly pinch the left corner of the form. Open point B so it forms a kite shape, then inside-reverse fold it so it tucks inside the form. When this step is complete, it should look like the illustration B.

a.

b.

4 Now make a crease at the dotted line as shown. Again, open point B. This time, push down on the area above the crease you just made (the area that looks like the top of the kite). At the same time, pull point B up, tucking it back into the body of the form. Turn your form over, and you can start to see the head and body of your cat.

5 Make two creases as shown. Then poke your finger at the point where the two creases meet and do a squash fold to form the fearsome feline's head.

a.

b.

6 The two points on either side are the cat's ears, which you must first fold down in valley folds. Then use a mountain fold to fold the top of the head back, and complete the ears by lifting the two points back up.

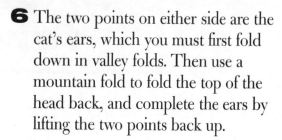

a.   b.   c.

7 Tuck the point at the bottom of the cat's face under.

8 Use puff paint to make the cat's eyes, nose, whiskers, and mouth. Glue on large white fangs cut from paper. Lay a pencil at the end of the tail and curl it tightly, then pull the pencil out.

a.

b.

TERRIFYING TIP

The Ferocious Feline Fiend is the perfect companion for the Flying Witch on page 22. But why not make the witch the black cat's little pet? Just make an extra-large cat and a smaller witch. Set the pair on a table or desktop to give all your visitors the heebie-jeebies.

HAUNTED forest

Make your own freaky forest with trees that die right before your eyes (almost).

WHAT YOU'LL NEED

brown origami paper • brown crayon • black marker
small twigs with tiny green leaves • glue

DIRECTIONS

1 First, you'll need to make the trunk of the tree. Start with Basic Form 1, then fold the upper right and left sides to the center line.

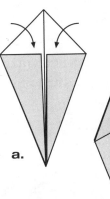

2 Fold the form in half, bringing the bottom to meet the top.

3 Fold it in half again by bringing the right side to the left.

4 Make a branch by opening the form slightly and pulling down on the inside flap so it sticks straight out like an arm. Your tree trunk is complete.

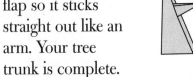

5 Use a black marker to draw a hauntingly scary face on your tree trunk. Make the mouth look like a big knot in the tree. Give the bark a rough, weathered look by rubbing the side of a brown crayon over the surface of the paper.

6 To give your tree leaves, gather small twigs with green leaves. Dip the bottom third of each twig in glue, then insert it into the folds of the top of the tree so it's secure and the leaves reach upward. As your tree gets older, the leaves will turn brown and die.

TERRIFYING TIP

These trees can make spooky place settings at your next party. Make the trees about a week before the get-together. Cut 3-by-5-inch index cards into smaller squares, and write each guest's name on a card. Stick each card into the branches of a tree, and place a tree next to each table setting.

CREEPO casket

A comfortable bed is essential for a good night's sleep.
This coffin will ensure pleasant dreams for all eternity.

WHAT YOU'LL NEED

two pieces of black or brown origami paper • black or brown marker
cotton balls • tape

DIRECTIONS

1 Begin with Basic Form 6. Fold the left inside flap to the left edge, then fold the right inside flap to the right edge. Turn the form upside down.

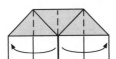

2 Use a valley fold to bring the far left side (front flap only) to meet the first crease. Repeat this with the front flap on the right side. Turn the form over and repeat this step.

3 To make the sides of your coffin, fold the top edge down as shown. It will just touch the two triangles in the corners. Then fold it over again, rolling it over the top of the triangles.

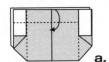 **a.**   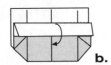 **b.**

4 Tuck each end of the flap underneath into a triangle so it's snug. Repeat this step and Step 3 on the other side.

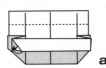 **a.**   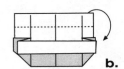 **b.**

5 Carefully hold the two longer sides and stretch them apart, and the bottom of the coffin will lift up on its own. Then firmly pinch the paper together to make sharp creases on each side.

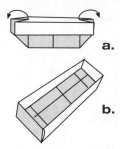

6 Make a lid for your coffin by using a slightly larger piece of paper (at least ½ inch all the way around) and following Steps 1–5.

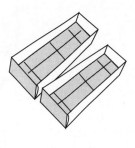

7 Attach the lid to the coffin with two small pieces of tape at the hinge points. You may want to color the exposed white areas with black or brown marker. To make an extra-soft bed for the newly deceased, spread out a few cotton balls and lay them in the bottom of the coffin.

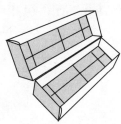

TERRIFYING TIP

At your next spooky party, make a casket for each guest and fill it with yogurt-covered pretzels for old skeleton bones!

GUTLESS Fred

Something has been eating at Fred, and now he's dead.

WHAT YOU'LL NEED

origami paper • scissors • markers • red pipe cleaners • tiny dried flower

DIRECTIONS

1 Begin with Basic Form 5. With the open end facing up, fold the upper edges on the right and left sides (front flaps only) to the center.

2 Now fold point A toward the left edge and point B toward the right edge. Unfold both. Lift the left "arm" of the triangle, open it slightly, and press down on point A to flatten it, then repeat this step with point B.

3 Turn the form over, and repeat Steps 1 and 2 on the other side.

a.   b.

4 Now you are ready to grasp point C (front flap only) and use a mountain fold to fold it back into the center. Repeat this step with point D, then turn the form over and repeat this step on the opposite side.

a.   b.   c.

5 Using valley folds, fold the top one-third and the bottom one-third to the center to make creases. Unfold.

6 At the top of your form are four open points. To make Fred come alive, take the shape, grasp the two outer points, and pull outward. Now flatten the base into a box shape.

a. b.

7 Take one flap and fold it back. Then take the tip of the point and fold it back as well. This will be Fred's head.

8 On the flap opposite the head, use scissors to cut a line up Fred's trousers so he has two legs, then fold the tips of each of these points outward to form feet.

a.

b.

9 The other two flaps are Fred's arms. Fill his belly with red, knotted pipe cleaners, then fold the flaps over to cover his insides. Use markers to draw sleeves and hands. Glue a dried flower in one hand to look like he's sleeping peacefully in his grave.

DECAYED bouquet

Wilted flowers are how ghouls say they care enough to give the very deadest.

WHAT YOU'LL NEED

black origami paper and purple origami paper • glue stick
pipe cleaners • red ribbon • scissors

DIRECTIONS

1 Glue a sheet of black origami paper to a sheet of purple origami paper, so that one side is black and the other side is purple.

2 Begin with Basic Form 5, with the open side pointing away from you, then fold the left and right points (front flaps only) to the center.

3 Now use a mountain fold to fold the left point back to touch the left edge and the right point back to touch the right edge, make creases, and unfold.

4 Turn the form over and repeat Steps 2 and 3 on the other side.

5 Your form should now have four flaps, two on each side. For this step, do an inside-reverse fold on one of the flaps by tugging it open slightly, then poking it into the body of the form. Repeat this step on each of the other three flaps.

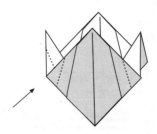

6 Use your scissors to cut across the bottom of your flower to make a very small hole.

7 Gently fold each petal out and curl them back. That's one flower—now make as many as you need for your decayed bouquet.

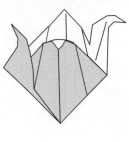

8 Poke a pipe cleaner through the hole in the bottom of each flower for a stem, and tape it in place. Bend each pipe cleaner so the flower looks wilted and droopy. Tie the flowers together with blood-red ribbon.

TERRIFYING TIP

Instead of a vase, let bodiless hands hold your decayed bouquet by stuffing gloves with tissue paper, then forming the fingers around the flowers.

ALIEN monster

Use metallic paper to fold up a space creature that's out of this world.

WHAT YOU'LL NEED

metallic origami paper • bobby pin • tape • paint or markers
white button • glue

DIRECTIONS

1 Begin with Basic Form 3, then turn your form over.

2 Fold each of the corners to the center.

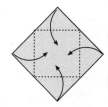

3 Turn the form over again, and just like you did in the last step, fold each of the corners to the center. Now that your form is getting smaller, it's harder to fold, isn't it?

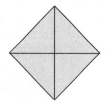
a.

b.

4 Turn your form over one more time, putting it in a diamond shape, and squash-fold the point at the bottom so it forms a rectangle. To do this, pull the two sides apart from the center opening and push down. You've just made your alien's pants.

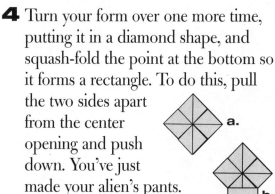
a.

b.

5 Now squash-fold the point on the left to form an arm. To make the arm look like it's reaching up in the air, push up on the bottom corner and do an inside-reverse fold to tuck it inside the sleeve.

6 Repeat Step 5 on the point on the right, but this time push down on the top corner so that the arm looks like it's reaching down.

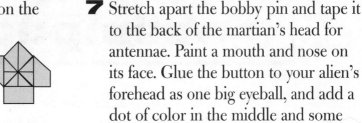

7 Stretch apart the bobby pin and tape it to the back of the martian's head for antennae. Paint a mouth and nose on its face. Glue the button to your alien's forehead as one big eyeball, and add a dot of color in the middle and some big, black lashes.

TERRIFYING TIP

The top half of a clear container from a gumball machine prize makes a great helmet for your space alien—just set it on top of his antennae to hold it in place.

GOBBLING
goblin puppet

While this creature may be made of paper,
it has a fearsome appetite for human flesh.

WHAT YOU'LL NEED

origami paper • flesh-colored construction paper or magazine • scissors
glue • round white stickers • markers • a drinking straw • tape

DIRECTIONS

1 Start with Basic Form 2, so that the two points meet at the bottom of the form. Then unfold the two bottom points so your form is in the shape of a triangle.

2 Fold the top left and right corners to the center, keeping the top edges aligned. Turn the form over.

3 Use a valley fold to fold the top left and right corners to meet the crease line. At the same time pull the flaps up from behind to the front. These are your goblin's ears. Turn the form over again.

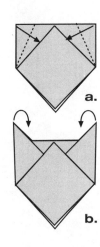

4 Use a mountain fold to fold the top layer (only) of the bottom point under about 1½ inches, and a valley fold to fold the under layer forward enough to be tucked underneath the top layer.

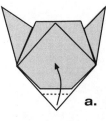

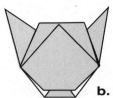

5 Paste on round stickers for eyes, coloring them in to look bloodshot. From flesh-colored construction paper, cut out two pieces of paper in the shape of legs, about 6 inches long (or you can cut a model's legs out of a magazine).

6 Glue the legs inside the monster's mouth so the torso appears to be gobbled down the goblin's throat and the legs stick out. Tape a drinking straw to the back of your goblin, allowing the straw to hang down at least 3 to 6 inches.

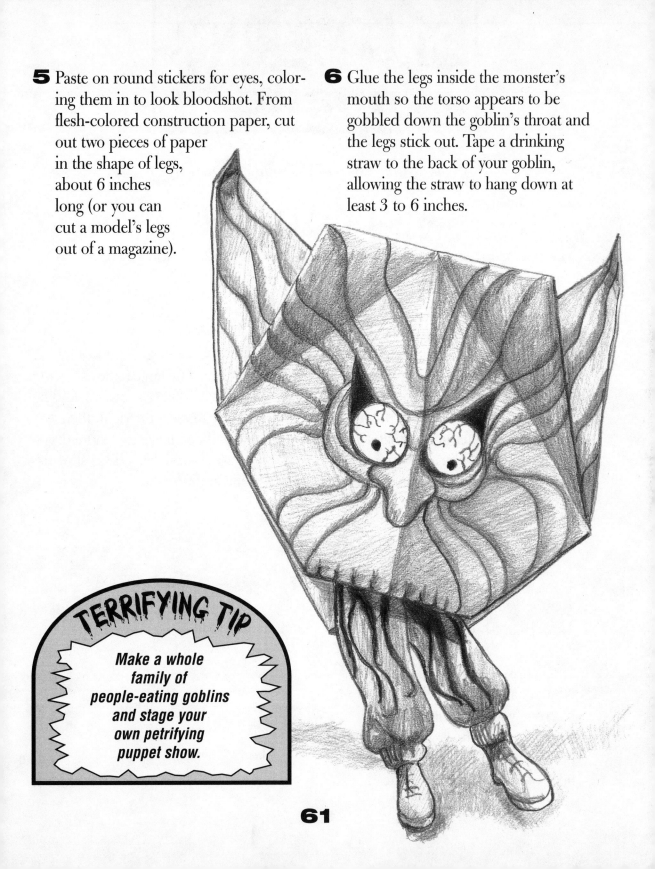

TERRIFYING TIP

Make a whole family of people-eating goblins and stage your own petrifying puppet show.

SLITHERING snake

Slippery, slimy, slinking . . . and oh, so savage!

WHAT YOU'LL NEED

fourteen 2-inch squares of origami paper • markers • glue • red ribbon

DIRECTIONS

1 Begin by making the snake's head. Crease a square of paper by folding the top half to the bottom edge, then unfolding. Fold the upper right corner down to the center line so that it forms a diagonal line to the upper left corner. Do a similar fold on the lower right corner, bringing it up to meet the center line.

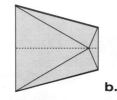

2 Now fold the top edge to meet the bottom edge. The larger side should be on the left. Make a crease by folding the left side to meet the right, then unfolding. Then make two more diagonal creases on the left side as shown in the illustration.

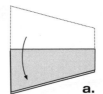
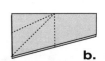

3 Now squash-fold the left side by inserting your finger into the flap's opening, lifting, and pressing it flat. That's the neck portion of the snake's head.

4 Make diagonal folds as shown, and squash-fold the right side to form the snake's face. The face and neck should just touch in the center.

5 Form fangs by folding down the two corners on the head.

6 Ready to make the body of the snake? Begin by making thirteen complete UFO pieces (described on page 40). Take one of the pieces and raise the left flap (the one with the fold, not the two separate corners), then squash-fold it so it forms a kite shape. That's it! Do the same on twelve of the pieces. The thirteenth UFO piece is for the tail.

a.

b.

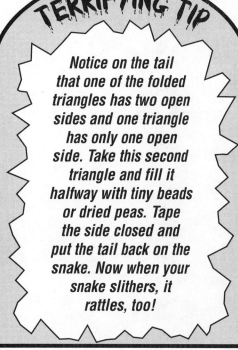

TERRIFYING TIP

Notice on the tail that one of the folded triangles has two open sides and one triangle has only one open side. Take this second triangle and fill it halfway with tiny beads or dried peas. Tape the side closed and put the tail back on the snake. Now when your snake slithers, it rattles, too!

7 To connect your snake's body, insert the folded point of one piece into the squash-folded pocket of another. Start with the head, add body parts, and finish up with the tail. Hold each in place with a dab of glue.

8 Cut out a thin triangle on the end of a piece of red ribbon to create a forked tongue. Attach this ribbon in between the fangs, and decorate the snake with beady yellow eyes and clammy scales.